Snap books™

Girls Got Game

girls' SNOWBOARDING

Showing Off Your Style

by Heather E. Schwartz

Consultant
Anthony Crute
Director/Head Coach
Pro Ride Snowboard Camps
Whistler, British Columbia, Canada

Capstone press®

Mankato, Minnesota

Snap Books are published by Capstone Press,
151 Good Counsel Drive, P.O. Box 669, Mankato, Minnesota 56002.
www.capstonepress.com

Library of Congress Cataloging-in-Publication Data
Schwartz, Heather E.
    Girls' snowboarding: showing off your style / Heather E. Schwartz.
    p. cm.—(Snap books. Girls got game)
    Summary: "Describes snowboarding, the skills needed for it, and ways
to compete"—Provided by publisher.
    Includes bibliographical references and index.
    ISBN-13: 978-1-4296-0135-1 (hardcover)
    ISBN-10: 1-4296-0135-3 (hardcover)
    1. Snowboarding—Juvenile literature. 2. Sports for women—Juvenile
literature I. Title. II. Series.
GV857.S57S34 2008
796.93'9082—dc22   2007000901

Editors: Kendra Christensen and Becky Viaene
Designer: Bobbi J. Wyss
Photo Researchers: Charlene Deyle and Scott Thoms

Photo Credits:
BigStockPhoto.com/Jacob, 18–19; Capstone Press/Karon Dubke, 6–7, 8, 9, 10–11, 22–23; Comstock, Inc., back cover;
Corbis/epa/Alessandro Della Bella, 21; Corbis/epa/Olivier Maire, 5; Corbis/NewSport/Steve Boyle, 26, 29; Corbis/Reuters, 28;
Fotolia/steba, 17; Getty Images Inc./AFP/FABRICE COFFRINI, cover; Getty Images Inc./Staff/Clive Mason, 24–25;
Hot Shots Photo, 32; iStockphoto/Ben Blakenburg, 13; iStockphoto/Ian McDonnell, 15 (top); Rex USA/Stewart Cook, 27;
SuperStock, Inc./Fogstock LLC, 14–15 (bottom);

Capstone Press thanks Mount Kato in Mankato, Minnesota, and Seth Yocum for their assistance with this book.
The publisher does not endorse products whose logos may appear on objects in images in this book.

1 2 3 4 5 6 12 11 10 09 08 07

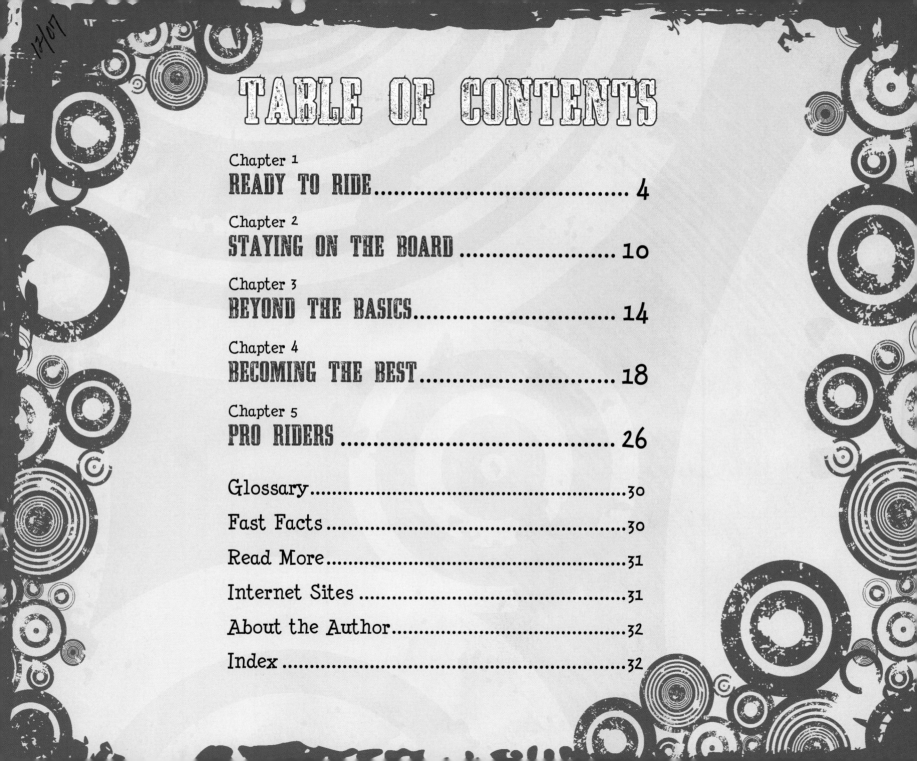

TABLE OF CONTENTS

CHAPTER ONE

READY TO RIDE

Picture yourself sailing through the air like snowboarder Hannah Teter in the 2006 Olympics. The crowd goes wild as you do your tricks and jumps. Your winning performance has just earned you a gold medal.

Doing tricks and jumps or developing control and speed takes plenty of practice. Snowboarders work hard at perfecting their skills. But even experienced snowboarders know that enjoying themselves is just as important as improving their skills. Once you start riding, you'll see why snowboarders just can't get enough of this sport.

Hannah
Teter

torino 2006

Shaping Up for Snowboarding

A few months before you step on a snowboard, you'll want to get your body ready. Snowboarding is an intense sport. It uses many of your muscle groups, so remember to stretch.

Along with stretching, you'll need to shape up. Lunges and jumping rope will help you strengthen your legs. Push-ups will give you strong arms to help you get up quickly from falls. Biking and jogging are also great ways to prepare your body for hours on the slopes.

Getting Your Gear

Ready to start snowboarding? Not so fast. First you'll need to bundle up. The best way to stay warm while snowboarding is to wear layers. Start with long underwear, socks, and a long-sleeved shirt that draws away sweat. Next, add a warm sweater or vest. Finish your outfit with a waterproof jacket, hat, snow pants, and gloves.

And don't forget to wear the things that help you stay safe. Add a helmet and goggles to your outfit. Grab the sunscreen. Even though it's cold out, your skin can still burn.

Studying the Signs

Before you cruise down the hill, you should know your way around. You can figure out which trails to hit by reading a map and looking for signs. On most hills in North America, beginner trails are marked with green circles, intermediate trails with blue squares, and expert trails with black diamonds. In Europe, green and blue are used for beginner trails, red marks intermediate trails, and black marks expert trails.

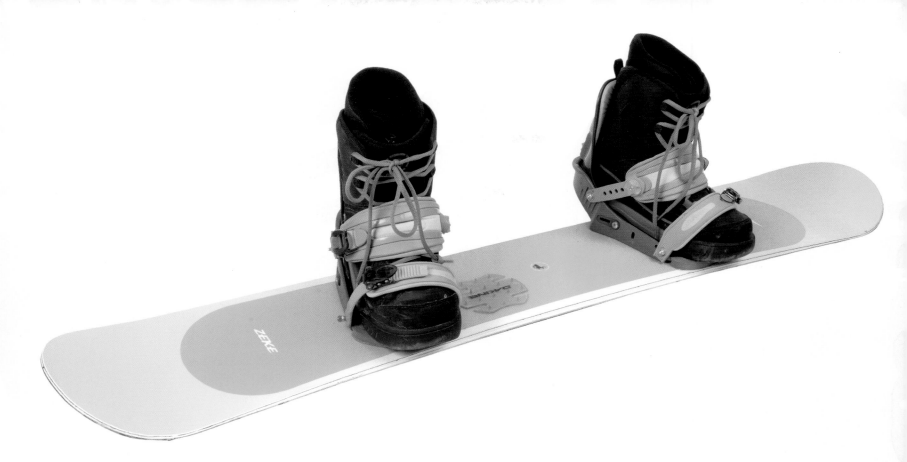

Boots and Board

Now you're ready for the most important parts of your outfit—the boots and the board. Find boots that fit snugly. Then decide if you want your left or right foot forward on the board. If you're more comfortable with your left foot forward, you're called regular foot. Snowboarders who prefer their right foot forward are called goofy foot. But no matter which foot you put first, you might feel a little awkward when you first begin!

CHAPTER TWO

STAYING ON THE BOARD

As a beginning snowboarder, your goal is to stay up on your board. An instructor can teach you how to do that—and more.

In your first few lessons, you'll focus on basic skills like balancing. Beginners also learn a basic move called skating. To skate, use the front binding to strap your forward foot to the board. Then use your other foot to push off and glide.

As you improve, you'll learn how to turn by shifting your weight and using the edges of the board. If you fall, don't worry. Getting up off the ground is a skill that any girl can learn.

“ My earliest (snowboarding) memory
was when I first learned to turn,
and my brother was there
cheering me on.

—Lindsey Jacobellis

2006 Olympic silver medalist in snowboardcross

Tricks to Try

Once you're traveling smoothly down the trail, you can experiment with tricks. Start with basic tricks, such as a fakie or an ollie.

A fakie is simply riding backward. To do this trick, turn so that your front foot is in the back.

Are you almost ready for a big jump? Start small with an ollie. Get speed, bend down, and then shift your weight to the back of the board. This trick will raise your board and let you jump a couple of inches off the ground.

These easy tricks won't seem so easy at first. But with lots of practice, you'll be ready to take your boarding to the next level.

Speeding Down the Slopes

Do you have a need for speed? Once you feel comfortable, you may want to pick up the pace. But make sure that wherever you're riding, you're always in control.

CHAPTER THREE

BEYOND THE BASICS

From high-flying moves to daring tricks, there is never a dull moment at a terrain park. This action-packed part of a mountain usually has a steep snow-covered ramp, called a halfpipe. Rails, boxes, and jumps also make terrain park riding more challenging. As you gain experience at terrain parks, you'll perform with standout style. Show everyone what you've got!

15

Tough Tricks

Experienced riders have no problem wowing crowds with their tough tricks. Once you've got the basics down, you can start practicing the more difficult moves.

Get ready to spin, 360-style. You'll start by flying off a halfpipe. Then you'll spin your body all the way around in the air. Soon you'll be craving more spinning action. Try the 540, which is one and a half spins, or the 720, which is two full spins.

After spinning, use the halfpipe for a hand plant. This move takes strength. Put one or both hands on the halfpipe wall, kick your legs and board above your head, and freeze.

“Women's snowboarding has progressed a lot. The younger riders are really pushing the limits of technical tricks. Their floor is our ceiling. It's awesome to be a part of it.

—Kelly Clark

2002 Olympic gold medalist in halfpipe

17

CHAPTER FOUR

BECOMING THE BEST

There's only one sure way to become a better snowboarder—ride as much as you can. Some girls take extra lessons to learn more advanced skills, like carving and handling bumps. You can take lessons individually or with a group. Snowboard clinics and camps also teach advanced moves.

"There are so many things that lead an athlete to success... for some it's all about effort and commitment, for others it's all about having a drive to achieve, and I feel like for me it's all about living in the moment.
–Hannah Teter
2006 Olympic gold medalist in halfpipe

Individual Competitions

Individual competitions are a great time to use your advanced moves against other riders. Many snowboard and ski areas hold competitions that are run by the United States of America Snowboard Association (USASA). At these competitions, snowboarders are divided into groups by age and event.

Most events are divided into alpine and freestyle. Alpine includes slalom. For slalom events, snowboarders race to the bottom of the hill while moving around obstacles. Alpine events are judged on speed and timing. Every hundredth of a second counts when you're trying to beat the clock!

Freestyle events include halfpipe and slopestyle. On the halfpipe, riders perform jumps and difficult tricks. For slopestyle, snowboarders use the halfpipe and obstacles like rails and picnic tables.

In freestyle events, you'll only have about 90 seconds to perform tricks with style and grace. Five judges rate you from 0.1 to 10.0. You'll get high points for doing difficult moves, having good form and style, and flying high in the air.

Snowboardcross is a mix between alpine and freestyle. Four to six riders race around obstacles until they reach the finish line at the bottom of the mountain. No matter which events you choose, there's a lot to think about when you compete, so stay focused.

Joining a Team

Do you want to combine competition with fun and friends? Join a snowboarding team. Some snowboard areas and high schools have teams. When you join a team, you'll get a chance to make new friends who share your love for snowboarding. You'll also get extra practice and coaching, so you'll be ready for team competitions.

Like individual competitions, team competitions include alpine and freestyle events. Judging is also similar to individual competitions. But all the team members' scores are added together for a final score. The team with the highest score wins.

You can rack up big points for your team by including many difficult and different moves. But it isn't just about winning. Team competitions can also motivate you to do your personal best.

The Next Level

Ready to take your riding to the next level? If you're winning at local and regional snowboarding competitions, try spinning, flipping, and jumping at national competitions.

Some day you may even be showing off your super skills at the Winter X Games. Only the most extreme and skilled snowboarders are invited to compete in the X Games. The best of the best also compete at the Winter Olympics. At the Olympics, female snowboarders compete in three events: the halfpipe, parallel giant slalom, and snowboardcross.

CHAPTER FIVE

PRO RIDERS

Some of the best snowboarders in the world are young women. Here's how they took their love of the sport all the way to the top.

Gretchen Bleiler originally wanted to go to the Olympics as a swimmer, diver, or hockey player. It turned out that snowboarding was her sport. In 2006, Bleiler won an Olympic silver medal in halfpipe.

Gretchen Bleiler

Hannah Teter

Snowboarding runs in Hannah Teter's family. She grew up with four older brothers who snowboard, and two of them are professionals. Teter even has a 6-foot (1.8-meter) skate ramp in her yard. In the summer, she stays in shape for snowboarding by skateboarding, wakeboarding, and playing soccer. Staying in shape and hours of practicing paid off. In 2006, Teter won an Olympic gold medal in the halfpipe event.

Kelly Clark

Kelly Clark started snowboarding at age 8. All her years of practice have paid off. Today, most female snowboarders can travel 5 to 6 feet (1.5 to 1.8 meters) in the air. Not Clark—she goes 8 to 9 feet (2.4 to 2.7 meters) in the air. No wonder she earned an Olympic gold medal in halfpipe in 2002! Clark offers some advice to girls just getting started in the sport. As she puts it, "Just keep remembering why you snowboard. There's a lot of stuff you can get caught up in, but step back and remember snowboarding's fun, but it also can be challenging. Remember the fun."

Lindsey Jacobellis' brother got her into snowboarding when she was 11. Today, she's an Olympic silver medalist in snowboardcross. She stays in shape for snowboarding by wakeboarding. She also likes riding ATVs on a backyard track and teaching kids how to snowboard.

Lindsey Jacobellis

No matter what your level is, start each snowboarding experience by imagining your success. By the time the snow melts, you'll have the control and speed you need for impressive tricks. Just imagine what you'll be able to do next winter!

GLOSSARY

alpine (AL-pine)—snowboarding that focuses on downhill racing

carving (CAR-ving)—slicing through the snow with the edge of the board

freestyle (FREE-stile)—snowboarding that focuses on tricks and jumps

halfpipe (HALF-pipe)—a snow-covered ramp used for performance of tricks and jumps

slalom (SLA-lom)—an individual alpine race around obstacles

slopestyle (SLOWP-stile)—a freestyle performance of tricks and jumps combined with an obstacle course

snowboardcross (SNOH-bord-krawss)—a mix between alpine and freestyle in which a group of snowboarders race around obstacles

FAST FACTS

 Before the 1980s, most ski areas didn't allow snowboarding. Today, snowboarders are welcome almost anywhere.

 Snowboarding became an Olympic sport at the 1998 Olympic Games in Nagano, Japan.

 Olympic giant slalom snowboarders race down mountains at speeds of almost 50 miles (81 kilometers) per hour.

READ MORE

Barr, Matt, and Chris Moran.
Snowboarding. Extreme Sports.
Minneapolis: Lerner, 2004.

Herran, Joe, and Ron Thomas.
Snowboarding. Action Sports.
Philadelphia: Chelsea House, 2003.

Preszler, Eric. *Snowboarding.* X-Sports.
Mankato, Minn.: Capstone Press, 2005.

Woods, Bob. *Snowboarding.* Kids'
Guides to Extreme Sports. Chanhassen,
Minn.: Child's World, 2005.

INTERNET SITES

FactHound offers a safe, fun way to
find Internet sites related to this book.
All of the sites on FactHound have been
researched by our staff.

Here's how:

1. Visit *www.facthound.com*

2. Choose your grade level.

3. Type in this book ID **1429601353** for
   age-appropriate sites. You may also
   browse subjects by clicking on letters,
   or by clicking on pictures and words.

4. Click on the **Fetch It** button.

**Facthound will fetch the best sites
for you!**

ABOUT THE AUTHOR

Heather E. Schwartz lives in upstate New York near some great mountains for snowboarding and skiing. She recently took up alpine skiing and loves the challenge of learning a new sport. Heather enjoys skiing with her husband, Philip, a lifelong skier.

When she's not skiing, Heather spends most of her time writing. She writes mainly about sports, fitness, health, animals, and other topics that interest kids. Her articles have appeared in *National Geographic Kids, Girls' Life, Teen,* and *All About You* magazines.

INDEX